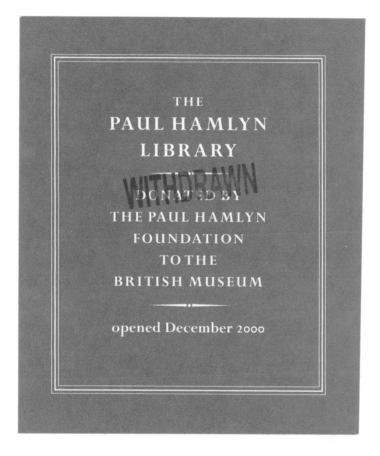

weblinks

You don't need a computer to use this book. But, for readers who do have access to the Internet, the book provides links to recommended websites which offer additional information and resources on the subject.

You will find weblinks boxes like this on some pages of the book.

weblinks

For more information about Judaism, go to www.waylinks.co.uk/ series/21stcentury/Judaism

waylinks.co.uk

To help you find the recommended websites easily and quickly, weblinks are provided on our own website, **waylinks.co.uk**. These take you straight to the relevant websites and save you typing in the Internet address yourself.

Internet safety

↗ Never give out personal details, which include: your name, address, school, telephone number, email address, password and mobile number.

↗ Do not respond to messages which make you feel uncomfortable – tell an adult.

↗ Do not arrange to meet in person someone you have met on the Internet.

↗ Never send your picture or anything else to an online friend without a parent's or teacher's permission.

↗ If you see anything that worries you, tell an adult.

A *note to adults*
Internet use by children should be supervised. We recommend that you install filtering software which blocks unsuitable material.

Website content

The weblinks for this book are checked and updated regularly. However, because of the nature of the Internet, the content of a website may change at any time, or a website may close down without notice. While the Publishers regret any inconvenience this may cause readers, they cannot be responsible for the content of any website other than their own.

HODDER
Wayland

21ST Century Judaism

Michael Keene

HODDER
Wayland

an imprint of Hodder Children's Books

First published in 2005 by Hodder Wayland,
an imprint of Hodder Children's Books

Consultant: Jonathan Gorsky, The Council of Christians
and Jews
Project Editor, Hodder Wayland: Kirsty Hamilton
Editor: Nicola Barber
Designer: Janet McCallum
Picture Researcher: Shelley Noronha, Glass Onion Pictures
Maps and artwork: Peter Bull

British Library Cataloguing Publication Data
Keene, Michael
Judaism – (21st century religions)
1. Judaism – Juvenile literature
I. Title
296

ISBN 075024707X

Colour Reproduction by Dot Gradations Ltd, UK
Printed in China

Hodder Children's Books
A division of Hodder Headline Limited
338 Euston Road, London NW1 3BH

The publisher would like to thank the following for permission
to reproduce their pictures: Art Directors/I. Genut 24;
Bridgeman Art Library www.bridgeman.co.uk/West London
Synagogue, UK 10, Palazzo Ducale, Urbino, Italy 13, Stapleton
Collection, UK 14, Private Collection 25; CIRCA Photo
Library/ Barrie Searle 18, 19, 26, 29; Corbis/David Rubinger
9, Hanan Isachar 39, Alexander Demianchuk/Reuters 43,
Reuters 45; Eye Ubiquitous 7; Jewish Museum, Berlin/Jens
Ziehe 41; Robert Harding Picture Library/S. Grandadam 15,
ASAP 21, A. Simmenauer 33, Photri 35; Hutchison Picture
Library 5; Alex Keene 23; Ann and Bury Peerless 8, 20; Zev
Radovan 28, 36, 44; Topfoto 4, 16, 17, 22, 27, 30, 31, 32, 34,
37, 38, 42

Contents

Note

In the Western world, years are numbered as either BC ('Before Christ') or AD (Anno Domini – which is Latin for 'In the year of our Lord…'). In this book, the more neutral terms BCE ('Before the Common Era') and CE ('Common Era') are used. The Jewish calendar gives the year of creation as 3760BCE. This means that the year 2000CE was 5760-5761 in the Jewish calendar.

Introduction

The Jewish community goes back thousands of years and today is to be found in most parts of the world. For many Jews, the feeling of belonging to this community is as important as the sense of sharing a common history with others. In Israel, a Jew is someone who is born to a Jewish mother or who converts to Judaism. Elsewhere, in Conservative and Reform Judaism (see page 8), children may be raised as Jewish if either parent belongs to the faith.

The Jewish 'family'

To understand the worldwide Jewish community of just over 13 million people, it helps to think of all Jews as belonging to one, very large 'family'. The members of this 'family' are part of one of the oldest religions in the world, a religion which began over three thousand years ago. They have not, however, always been known by this name. In the beginning, Jews were known as 'Israelites' from their ancestor, Jacob (also called Israel). Then they were called 'Hebrews' after the nomadic tribe of which they were a part. These two names were later linked to the language that they spoke (Hebrew) and the country in which they lived (Israel). The word 'Jew' comes from 'Judah', the name of one of the tribes descended from Jacob. Most of these tribes disappeared more than two thousand five hundred years ago, when they were exiled from their homeland (see page 12), but the 'Judeans' later returned.

Belonging to this Jewish 'family' means accepting a whole way of life with its own religious and cultural traditions, including special dietary laws and customs. Just like any large family, the Jewish family is made up of people with very different opinions, who like to live and worship in different ways. Some, called 'secular Jews', do not actively worship God but may nevertheless feel themselves to be part of the Jewish community.

◄ A Jewish child lights the last candle on a special eight-branched candlestick that is used during the festival of Hanukkah (see page 34).

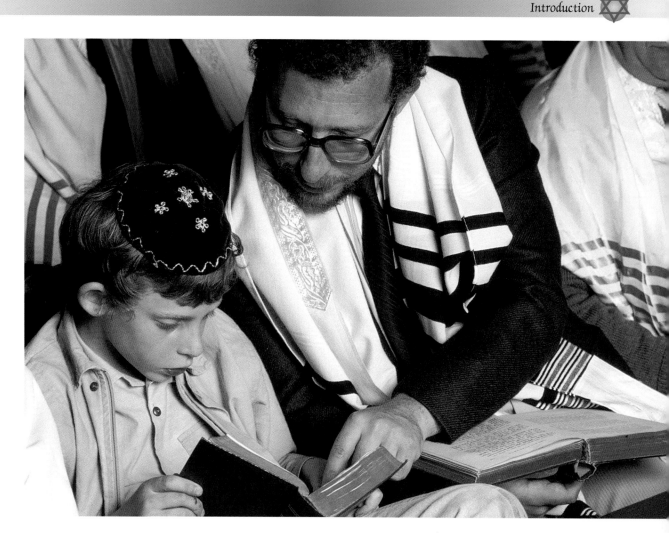

▲ A father and son sit together during worship in a synagogue in London, UK. The father is wearing his tallit (prayer shawl), as he does every time he prays in the synagogue (see page 30), and his son has a kippah (skullcap) on his head.

In our own words

"All Jews are part of a long, and very proud, religious tradition. We feel a link with all the Jews who have lived, and suffered, back to the time of our father, Abraham. There is no single Jewish way that we all follow. We do what suits us individually in the end. The bottom line is that you do what feels right. To describe Judaism as a 'family' is right. We sometimes have strong disagreements with other members of the 'family' and fall out, but it rarely lasts. I have yet to meet anyone who is not, deep down, proud to be a Jew."

Deborah, aged 16, UK

Where are Jews found?

Throughout history Jews have always moved around, often as refugees searching for a new home. As a result they have, over the centuries, settled in most parts of the world.

The Ashkenazim and the Sephardim

There are two main Jewish traditions the *Ashkenazim* and the *Sephardim*. The Ashkenazim refers to Jews from central and eastern Europe. These Jews originally lived in northern France and Germanic cities along the River Rhine. The name Ashkenazim comes from the Hebrew name *Ashkenaz* which became associated with an ancient Germanic tribe, the Ascanians, and therefore with the German Jews. The Ashkenazim created their own distinctive culture with their own language – *Yiddish*, a mixture of German and Hebrew. Today, most of the Jews living in the United States are descended from the Ashkenazim, and many others live in Israel and Australia.

The name Sephardim comes from the Hebrew word for Spain. It describes those Jews who were originally from Spain and Portugal, but who fled to North Africa, Greece, Italy and the Ottoman Empire after being expelled by the Christian rulers of Spain in 1492 (see page 15). Like the Ashkenazim, the Sephardim also had their own culture and their own language – *Ladino*, a mixture of Spanish and Hebrew.

These two Jewish groups have their own customs, traditions, liturgy, songs and prayers. At the same time, they share their most important beliefs.

▼ *This map shows the worldwide spread of the Jewish community.*

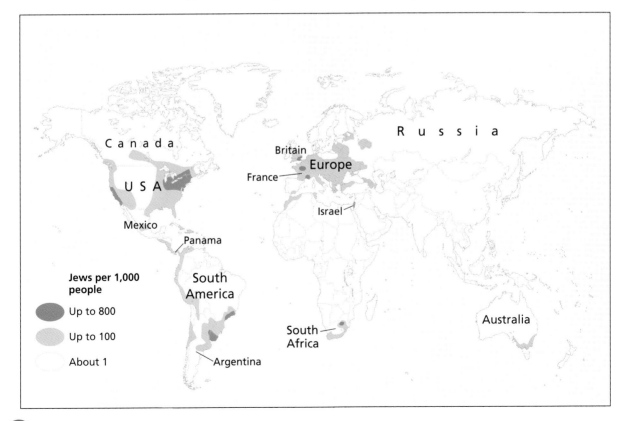

Jews per 1,000 people

Up to 800

Up to 100

About 1

The spread of the Jews

The largest Jewish community in the world is in the USA. There are 5.5 million American Jews, with almost 2 million of this number living in New York. There are about 4.5 million Jews living in Israel. There has always been a small Jewish community in Israel, but many European Jews started to move to Israel in the late 19th and early 20th centuries in response to poverty and persecution. More Jews arrived after the end of the Second World War (1939-45), and after the founding of the state of Israel (1948) people came from many different countries. Amongst them were Jews from Iran and Iraq in the late 1940s, and Jews from Ethiopia in the 1980s and 1990s. Jews from the Yemen started to settle in Israel as early as the 1880s, but this movement speeded up in the early 20th century and again after 1948. About 300,000 Jews now live in Great Britain, with about 200,000 of them in London and the southeast of England.

▲ *A shop front in the Jewish Quarter of the East Side in New York, USA. The city of New York has a larger Jewish population than any other city in the world.*

Jewish groups

Within Judaism there are three main groups: Orthodox, Progressive and Conservative Jews.

Orthodox Jews

Most Jews in Great Britain and Israel belong to an Orthodox synagogue. However, in the USA, Orthodox Jews account for only ten per cent of the Jewish population. Orthodox Jews believe that the *Torah*, the first five books of the Bible, is God's eternal word and can never change. In an Orthodox synagogue men and women sit separately, and the Hebrew language is used in all services. Women do not lead services in Orthodox synagogues. A *Bar Mitzvah* service is held for all boys at the age of 13 to mark their reception as adults into the Jewish community (see page 37). For weekday services, men wear the traditional *tefillin* (small leather boxes containing scriptural writings) on their forehead and left arm, as well as a skullcap and a prayer shawl. The Sabbath day is kept strictly as a day of rest, and the *kosher* rules about food (see pages 26-7) are followed throughout the week.

▲ *This man is wearing his tefillin and his son is carrying a Torah scroll. The occasion is the boy's Bar Mitzvah, which is being held at the Western Wall in Jerusalem (see page 15).*

each person, and that what is right for one person may not be right for another. Men and women sit together in Progressive synagogues, and services are conducted in the everyday language of worshippers. Women are allowed to be *rabbis*.

Progressive Jews

Most Progressive Jews belong to Reform or Liberal synagogues, although there are several other groups of Progressive Jews. Both Reform and Liberal Jews share a common belief that Judaism should adapt over time to suit changing circumstances. Progressive Judaism teaches that God guides and judges

Conservative Jews

The Conservative movement is very substantial in the USA and numerically small but lively in the UK. Conservative Jews are traditionally orthodox rather than 'progressive', while at the same time emphasizing the historical development and flexibility of the tradition.

➤ *Rabbi Naamah Kelman takes a service in 1992. While services in an Orthodox synagogue can only be taken by a male rabbi, women can be rabbis in the Progressive tradition. Naamah Kelman was the first female rabbi to be ordained in Israel, at the Hebrew Union College, Jewish Institute of Religion, in Jerusalem.*

Ten basic facts about Judaism

1 Judaism began more than 3,000 years ago in Mesopotamia, the region in the Middle East that is modern Iraq.

2 Jews worship one God.

3 There are about 13 million Jews in the world today.

4 A Jewish place of worship is called a synagogue.

5 The Torah is the most important part of the Scriptures.

6 The scrolls of the Torah, the most precious objects in a synagogue, sit in the Ark – a cupboard at the front of the synagogue.

7 The best-known Jewish symbols are the six-pointed Star of David and the seven-branched candlestick (the *menorah*).

8 Jews trace their ancestry back to Abraham, the father of their nation, and to Moses, who gave them their precious Torah.

9 The Sabbath day (*Shabbat*), which starts about half an hour before the beginning of sunset every Friday and is completed when the stars appear in the sky (dusk) on Saturday night, is a day of rest for all Jews.

10 Jews have their own calendar which goes back to what they believe is the day of creation. This calendar is 3,761 years ahead of the Western calendar.

Judaism can be traced all the way back to Abraham, who lived nearly four thousand years ago in roughly 1800BCE. He is referred to by Jews today as 'our father, Abraham', and is remembered as the person who began the Jewish people. Much later (see page 12), Moses gave the Jews their religious faith.

Abraham

Abraham was brought up in the small town of Ur, in southern Mesopotamia, close to the Persian Gulf. Like everyone else at the time, his family worshipped many gods. However, Abraham came to believe in one God who created the world and controlled human history. This event marks the beginning of Judaism. At about the same time, God made a promise to Abraham which marked out the Jews as God's 'Chosen People' – 'chosen' not because they were better than other people, but because they were different as a result of their relationship with God.

➤ *This painting, by a 20th-century artist, shows Abraham about to offer his son, Isaac, as a sacrifice. Jews believe that this was a test of Abraham's faith in God. The painting is in the West London Synagogue, UK.*

Patriarchs

Abraham was told by God to travel over 2,000 kilometres with his family to a new country, Canaan, now called Israel. God also promised that he would make a great nation out of Abraham's descendants. But Abraham and his wife, Sarah, remained childless until they were both quite old. Then Sarah gave birth to a son when she was well beyond normal child-bearing age. The child's name was Isaac. Jews believe that they are all descendants of Abraham, and he is known as a patriarch, or founding father, of their religion. Abraham's son, Isaac, and his grandson, Jacob, are also revered by Jews as patriarchs.

God's promise to Abraham

According to the Torah, the holy book of the Jews, this is God's promise to Abraham:

'I will make you a great nation
and I will bless you;
I will make your name great,
and you will be a blessing.
I will bless those who bless you,
and whoever curses you I will curse
and all peoples on earth
will be blessed through you.'

(Genesis 12:2-3)

▼ *This map shows the route taken by Abraham when he responded to the call of God to move his extended family to another country.*

Moses

Throughout history, Jews who are believed to have received messages from God have been called 'prophets'. The greatest of all the Jewish prophets was Moses, known to Jews as 'Moses, our teacher' (*Moshe Rabeinu* in Hebrew). Moses lived about 600 years after Abraham (see page 10).

Ten plagues

In about 1650BCE, the Israelites went to Egypt to find food after a famine in Canaan. But the Egyptian Pharaoh (king) treated them very badly, and forced them to work as slaves. By the time of Moses, the Israelites had been slaves in Egypt for over 400 years. Moses believed that God was calling him to lead the Israelites out of their slavery, and he told the Pharaoh that many disasters would fall on the Egyptians if the Pharaoh did not release the Israelites. When the Pharaoh refused, ten plagues hit Egypt – the rivers turned to blood;

plagues of frogs, lice and flies covered the land; all of the farm animals died; the people were covered with painful boils; there was a mighty hailstorm; a plague of locusts destroyed the crops; darkness covered the whole land for many days and, worst of all, the eldest son in every Egyptian family died.

These plagues were believed to be punishments from God. After the last one, the Pharaoh released his captives. It took the Israelites forty years to travel back to the land of Canaan (Israel). On this journey in the wilderness, known as the Exodus, the Israelites received some precious laws from God which were given to Moses on Mount Sinai. The most important of these laws are called the Ten Commandments.

▼ *This map shows the route taken by the Israelites when they left Egyptian slavery and travelled to the 'Promised Land' of Canaan. The journey took them 40 years to complete.*

The Ten Commandments

The Ten Commandments form the basis of the Jewish faith. They also contain laws that are followed by people in most societies. They are:

1 *I am the Lord your God. You must obey no other gods but me.*

2 *You must not make any idols to worship.*

3 *You must not use God's name carelessly.*

4 *You must remember to keep the Sabbath day holy.*

5 *You must respect your mother and father and obey them.*

6 *You must not murder.*

7 *You must not commit adultery*

8 *You must not steal.*

9 *You must not tell lies or spread rumours about other people.*

10 *You must not covet (want something that does not belong to you).*

▼ Moses proclaims the Ten Commandments which he received from God on Mount Sinai. The Commandments were written in Hebrew on stone tablets. This painting is by a 15th-century Dutch artist, Joos van Gent.

Later Jewish history

There were several tribes in Canaan, each one controlling a small part of the country, so there were many battles before the Israelites finally re-established themselves. The threat of warfare with one of these tribes, the Philistines, led the Israelites to choose a king, Saul, to lead them. He was followed by a succession of kings including David and Solomon, David's son. Solomon was famed for his great wisdom and he built a magnificent Temple in Jerusalem in which to worship God.

After Solomon died, Canaan was divided into two parts, Israel and Judah. The people who lived in Judah became known as Jews. In 722BCE Israel was conquered by the Assyrians and in 586BCE Judah fell to the Babylonians.

The old Temple was destroyed and the inhabitants of both countries were taken into exile, where they remained for centuries. The communities of Jews that settled outside Israel later became known as the *Diaspora*.

Over the following centuries, Jews gradually began to return to their homeland. In 63BCE Judah was occupied and ruled by the Romans. At first the Romans allowed the Jews religious freedom, but later they tried to crush Jewish power and influence. In 70CE they destroyed the rebuilt Jewish Temple and prevented the Jews from living in – or even entering – Jerusalem. They also outlawed

▼ *This 15th-century woodcut shows the walled city of Jerusalem with the Temple of Solomon at its centre. The illustration is by the German artist Hartmann Schedel.*

Jewish education and killed any Jews who continued to teach their young. Most of the Jews fled into exile again.

New lands

In the centuries that followed groups of Jews settled in many different countries. They were often mistrusted by their new neighbours and this mistrust frequently led to hatred and persecution. The Jews had only two things left from their history – their God and their traditions. These were not only important for religious reasons but also for Jewish pride and survival. To other people, however, they seemed dangerous and threatening.

Christian countries were often the worst places for Jews to live. Jews were persecuted by having their property confiscated, by expulsion, and sometimes by death. Jews were expelled from England, for example, in 1290 and from parts of France in 1306. Jews prospered in Muslim Spain for many centuries, but this was followed by a time of intolerance and oppression. In 1492, the Spanish Jews were given the choice by the Christian rulers of Spain either to convert to Christianity or to leave Spain. Thousands left – many to start a new life in Istanbul (in present-day Turkey), where they were welcomed by the Muslim Ottoman rulers. Some Jews, however, chose to stay in Spain and pretend that they were Christian converts. When the Christian authorities discovered what was happening they set up special courts called the Inquisition. These courts used torture and death to persuade Jews to give up their religious beliefs.

Persecution continued in the centuries that followed. For example, in the 19th century Russian Jewish families were often forced to leave their homes and settle elsewhere in hostile and dangerous parts of the country. All of this history forms the background to the unspeakable horrors that were visited on the Jewish people during the Holocaust in the 20th century.

weblinks
For more information about the Western Wall go to:
www.waylinks.co.uk/series/21stcentury/Judaism

The Temple of Solomon

The Temple that Solomon built in Jerusalem was magnificent. About 180,000 people were involved in its construction, and its dedication ceremony lasted for fourteen days. It was the place where the three most important Jewish festivals – Pesach, Sukkot *and* Shavuot *– were celebrated. It was destroyed in 586*BCE *although a much larger Temple, built by Herod the Great, replaced it until that, too, was destroyed in 70*CE*. The Temple has never been rebuilt.*

▲ *The only wall of Herod's Temple that still remains standing in Jerusalem is one of the holiest sites in Judaism. It is known as the Western Wall.*

The Holocaust

In Germany, in the 1930s, Jews once more faced persecution and danger. The Chancellor of Germany, Adolf Hitler, hated the Jews and used them as a convenient scapegoat to blame for every problem faced by his country.

Although persecution of Germany's Jewish population began before the Second World War (1939-45), Hitler's programme to rid his country and the world of all Jews was put into operation during the war. Hitler called this plan 'The Final Solution'.

Hitler's persecution of the Jews had several distinct stages. At first, all Jews had to register at a local office and wear a yellow Star of David on their clothes so that they could be easily identified. Then began an attack on the human rights and freedoms of Jews – their businesses were destroyed, their children were not allowed to go to school and

Jewish adults were not permitted to own cars. Jews were forced to move into ghettos, walled-in areas of towns and cities, where they lived in overcrowded conditions, often with insufficient food. Many Jews were sent to concentration camps, places of forced labour where thousands of people died from ill-treatment and lack of food. The final stage of Hitler's 'programme' saw Jews being rounded up and sent to death camps – places of mass murder.

By the end of the Second World War, six million Jews, including one million children, had been killed. This time of horrific persecution and death became known as the Holocaust – 'a time of raging fire'.

▼ *Jews in the ghetto in Warsaw, Poland, surrender to German soldiers after an uprising against the Nazis in 1943. About 40,000 Jews died during this rebellion.*

The State of Israel

During the 19th century, Jews had begun to resettle in their old homeland of Palestine. A group of Jews called Zionists began to campaign for a separate Jewish state to be set up within Palestine. The events of the Holocaust led to a renewed determination for this plan. On 14 May 1948 Palestine was divided up and the modern state of Israel was formed. Jews from all over the world began to travel to this new country to make their home there.

The creation of Israel out of Palestine inevitably led to hostility between Israelis and non-Jewish Palestinians (mainly Muslim Arabs), and between Israel and the surrounding countries, which were mainly

▲ *An Israeli soldier arrests a Palestinian demonstrator. Conflict between the Israelis and the Palestinians has continued since the State of Israel was set up in 1948.*

weblinks

For more information about the Holocaust, go to:
www.waylinks.co.uk/series/21stcentury/Judaism

Arab. The Israelis were not prepared to give up any of the land that they believed God had given them thousands of years ago. Most of the Arab countries did not even recognize the right of the state of Israel to exist. Efforts to find a lasting solution to the Arab-Israeli conflict continue today, but so far without any real success.

2 Beliefs and holy books

Jews believe in one, invisible, eternal God. They also believe that they have a special relationship with God and were chosen by him to receive the Torah. By studying its teachings and putting them into practice they hope to spread peace and justice in the world. Jews believe that life in this world is very precious, and that the destination of the journey of life is a life after death.

God

The first Hebrew that most Jewish children learn is the *Shema*, which is both a prayer and a statement of faith. The words of the Shema are taken from the Scriptures. They underline the Jewish belief that there is only one God who created the world and sees and knows everything. This God is close to everyone and everything. Jews have a word to describe this closeness – *Shekhina*. The *Talmud*, a Jewish holy book, says: 'There is no place without the Shekhina.' Jews repeat the Shema twice each day – first thing in the morning and last thing at night.

▼ *A Jewish woman shields her eyes as she prays, as a mark of respect to God.*

The Covenant

Jews have always believed that they have a special and unique relationship with God. According to the Jewish Scriptures this relationship is built on a covenant, or agreement, which was made between God and Abraham thousands of years ago. God promised to be Israel's God and give the Israelites a country of their own. In return God told the Israelites to dedicate themselves to him alone and his service and not to worship any other gods.

Later, God renewed this covenant with Abraham's son, Isaac, and with Isaac's son, Jacob who was also called Israel. Although the Jews are sometimes known as 'Chosen People' this special relationship is one of service, not privilege – Jews have been called by God to fulfil his commandments and to be a blessing to the world.

The Shema

The Shema is a combination of three passages taken from the Torah: 'Hear, O Israel, the Lord is our God. You shall love the Lord your God with all your heart, with all your soul and with all your mind. These words which I command you this day you shall take to heart. You shall teach them diligently to your children. You shall recite them when you are at home and when you are away, morning and night. You shall bind them as a sign on your hand, they shall be a reminder above your eyes and you shall inscribe them on the doorposts of your home and on your gates.'

weblinks

For an explanation of Jewish beliefs and what it means to be a Jew, go to:
www.waylinks.co.uk/series/21stcentury/Judaism

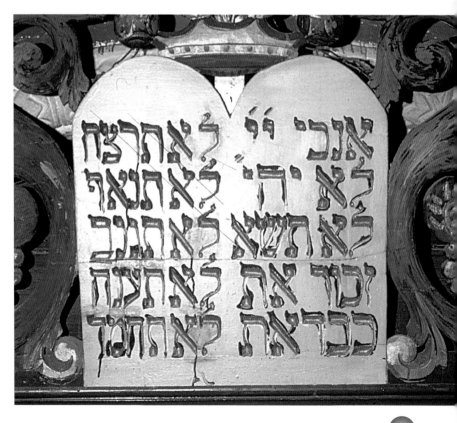

➤ *The Ten Commandments on the wall of a synagogue in Safed, Israel. They act as a reminder to every worshipper of the importance of these precious laws. They are written in Hebrew.*

'Teaching'

The word 'Torah' means 'teaching' – all the things that God has told the Jewish people – and it is at the heart of Jewish life and worship. The word refers primarily to the first five books of the Jewish Scriptures and contains stories about the early history of the Jewish people, commandments and rules, poems and sayings about life.

The Torah is divided into portions for each week of the year so that it is read in the synagogue in a never-ending cycle from beginning to end throughout the year. Studying the Torah is a very important part of Jewish life. The text of the Torah is the Jew's link with God. The role of the Jewish rabbi is to teach the Torah since it is both the source of holiness and eternal life.

▼ *When not in use, the scrolls of the Torah are stored in the Ark – a cupboard situated at the front of every synagogue. The scrolls are the most precious objects in a synagogue.*

The giving of the Torah

There is a much-loved Jewish legend which describes how, when the Torah was given to the people by God on Mount Sinai, the mountain itself burst into flower, the birds stopped singing and the whole universe became quiet and still – as if waiting for something very beautiful to happen. This was followed by thunder, lightning and a thick cloud which covered the whole mountain. God came down on to the mountain in fire and the area shuddered. Such is the power of the Torah.

▲ *The scrolls of the Torah are written out by hand by a specially trained scribe.*

The Messiah

The idea of the Messiah comes from the Jewish Bible. The word means 'the anointed one' and comes from the ancient practice of anointing kings with oil when they were crowned. The Bible looks forward to a new king for the Jews who will be even greater than the much-loved King David (see page 14). Orthodox Jews are still waiting for this king, who will make everything right on earth, while Progressive Jews look for a new age of love and peace. Many Jews pray each day for their Messiah to come.

The afterlife

The Bible teaches Jews how they should live in this life. But the Jewish Scriptures also make it clear that there is a life after death. They teach that when a person dies their soul survives in *Sheol*, a place of darkness and shadows. God will reward those who have lived a righteous life and punish those who have been sinners – both in this life and in the life beyond death. When God's promised Messiah comes to set up his kingdom on earth, then the righteous will be brought back to life.

The Jewish holy books

The Jewish Bible, or *Tenakh*, is the holy book for all Jews. The Tenakh is a very old collection of writings which falls into three sections: the Torah (teachings), the Prophets (*Nevi'im*), and the Writings (*Ketuvim*; songs and sayings). The sections are divided into different parts, called books. There are 39 books altogether in the Jewish Scriptures. The Torah, for instance, includes the five books of Genesis, Exodus, Leviticus, Deuteronomy and Numbers.

The Jewish Bible contains many different kinds of writing. It recounts the history of the Jews from the creation of the world to the time when they were exiled from their homeland of Israel. There are many songs, poems and wise sayings that arise from this story. But the main theme running through the Jewish Bible is how God loved and guided the Jews, saving them many times from their enemies but also punishing them when they deliberately disobeyed him. Alongside this is a record of the laws and rules which Jews try to follow to please God.

The Torah

The Jews value the first part of their Bible – the Torah – very highly. The books that make up the Torah are a mixture of early Jewish

▼ *A scroll of the Torah is spread out on the bimah in a synagogue in Havana, Cuba, to be read as part of worship. To read from the Torah is a great honour.*

◄ *This stained glass window in a synagogue in the UK illustrates the festival of Simchat Torah.*

weblinks

For more information about the Jewish Scriptures, go to:
www.waylinks.co.uk/series/
21stcentury/Judaism

history and laws. The Torah contains the stories about the creation of the world and early Jewish history ending with the death of Moses. It also has hundreds of rules covering such matters as cleanliness and diet, as well as the Ten Commandments (see page 13).

Simchat Torah

The annual festival of *Simchat Torah* gives Jews the opportunity to thank God for his great gift of the Torah to them. Over the course of the year the whole of the Torah, from start to finish, is read in the synagogue on the Sabbath day. Simchat Torah is the day when the last part of the last book, Deuteronomy, is read. The reading then starts again with the first chapter of the first book, Genesis. There is no break between the two readings to show that God's word, the Torah, is eternal, without beginning or end.

In our own words

"As a Jew the Torah means a great deal to me. The commandments that I find in the Torah are my everyday guide to living. I am able to identify with many of the characters in the Torah, especially Abraham and Moses. They strike me as being real people with many faults and their good points as well. I do not think that the Torah lays down impossible standards for me to reach. It tells me how I should treat other people as if they really matter. It lays down a way of life that I want to follow."

Rachel, aged 14, UK

The Prophets and the Writings

Although not as important as the Torah, the Prophets and the Writings are essential parts of the Jewish Scriptures.

The Prophets

A prophet was a human being, male or female, who had been chosen by God to act as his messenger and to make his will known to the people. A prophet was someone who spoke on God's behalf. Although the prophets sometimes made pronouncements about the future, they mostly spoke out about the evils of the present time which displeased God. Many of those evil deeds were being carried out by kings and religious leaders of the time, so the prophets needed great courage to challenge them. The term is also used of the Jewish prophets whose words and sayings can be found in the prophetic books of the Jewish Bible. These were people who declared God's judgement on human sin and his willingness to save and restore the fortunes of the obedient.

Some of the prophetic books take their name from the prophet whose message is in the book. For example, there are books named after Isaiah, Jeremiah and Ezekiel. The books of these prophets are long and important. There are also twelve books named after less important prophets such as Hosea, Obadiah, Jonah and Malachi. These books are much shorter.

◄ An engraving of the prophet Isaiah by the 19th-century French artist Gustav Doré, whose illustrations were often used in Jewish Bibles. This picture is in the Tel Aviv Museum in Israel.

The Writings

The Writings are a collection of poems, songs and wise sayings which make up the final part of the Tenakh. The most popular of these writings is the Book of Psalms, a collection of 150 songs that were used in worship in the Temple. King David and his son, Solomon, are believed to have written many of them. The psalms are notable for the honesty of their writers when they describe their feelings about God and their enemies. Another important book in the Writings is the Book of Proverbs, a collection of many wise sayings. King Solomon is also thought to be the author of many, if not all, of these.

From the Psalms

In this psalm the writer is bitter about God. He feels he has been deserted by the Almighty:

'My God, my God, why have you
    forsaken me?
Why are you so far from saving [me],
So far from the words of my
    groaning?
O my God, I cry out day by day, but
    you do not answer,
By night and am not silent.'
(Psalm 22:1,2)

In this psalm the writer shows a deep faith in God:

'The Lord is my shepherd, I shall not
    be in want.
He makes me lie down in green
    pastures
He leads me beside still waters,
He restores my soul.'
(Psalm 23:1-3)

▲ *King Solomon and the Queen of Sheba appear on this 19th-century Jewish rug, made in Kashan, Iran. Solomon became famous for his great wisdom and according to tradition wrote three books of the Jewish Bible – Ecclesiastes, the Book of Proverbs and the Song of Solomon.*

3 Worship, the synagogue and holy days

J ews do not have to go to the synagogue to worship God. They can express their faith in the way they live their everyday lives, especially in their family life, and in how they behave in the wider world. The way that Jews live is a very important part of belief and worship. They believe that life itself is a gift from God, and that everyday activities such as eating a meal or going to bed offer opportunities for praising God. It is said that for every human activity there is a Jewish prayer to be offered to God.

The mezuzah

The *mezuzah* is a tiny scroll made out of parchment on which is written the first two paragraphs of the Shema (see page 19). Mezuzah scrolls are placed inside small wooden or plastic casings and attached to the right-hand doorposts of every room in the house – apart from the bathroom and toilet. A mezuzah is also placed on the outside doorpost. As traditional Jews enter and leave their house they touch the mezuzah and kiss their fingers. This reminds them of the promise in the Torah: 'You are blessed when you come in and blessed when you go out.' (Deuteronomy 28:6)

Dietary laws

The word kosher means that which is 'allowed' or 'suitable'. Many Orthodox Jews eat only kosher food, but Progressive Jews may not be so strict. The laws that lay down

➤ *The mezuzah attached to the doorpost of a Jewish home is a reminder of the holiness of the house and God's presence in it.*

the restrictions observed by Jews are to be found in the Torah. The main restrictions are listed here:

- The meat of any animal that does not both chew the cud and have cloven hooves is forbidden. The best known example is the pig. Jews do not eat any sea creature that does not have fins and scales. Only birds known to be kosher, for example chicken, duck and turkey, are permitted.

- All animals have to be slaughtered according to strict laws, with all of the blood drained from the carcase before it can be eaten.

- Meat and milky foods must not be eaten together. It is the practice to wait for several hours before eating milky foods after meat has been eaten. Meat and milk are kept separately in the fridge and cooked in different containers.

In our own words

"I am not sure that I understand all of the kosher rules and the reasons for them. When I asked the rabbi at my synagogue to explain them to me he said that there were two reasons for the original rules. The first was to maintain a high level of hygiene when our ancestors were travelling across the desert. The second, and most important, is a matter of obedience to God. We may not understand everything that God tells us to do, but that is when we need to trust most strongly."

Anna, aged 15, USA

weblinks

For more information about the Jewish synagogue, go to:
www.waylinks.co.uk/series/
21stcentury/Judaism

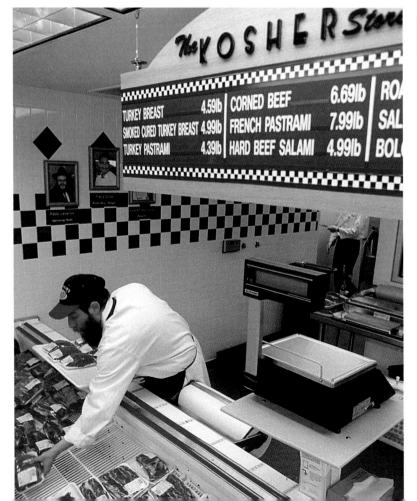

◄ *A kosher butcher in a department store in Austin, Texas, USA. Every kosher butcher's shop is examined by the Jewish religious authorities and given a certificate to state that its meat is kosher – fit to be eaten by Jews trying to keep to the dietary restrictions.*

Keeping the Sabbath day

Shabbat, the Sabbath day, is the Jewish holy day of rest and is the only weekly festival in Judaism. It reminds all Jews of two things: that God rested after creating the world in six days, and that God delivered the Israelites from slavery in Egypt (see page 12).

The Sabbath day

Each Jewish day of twenty-four hours starts at sunset in the evening and runs to sunset in the next evening. So the Jewish Sabbath begins on Friday evening and finishes at sunset on Saturday evening. On Friday, before the onset of the Sabbath, the house is cleaned and tidied and a special meal is prepared. When the Sabbath day begins no work of any kind is allowed. The meal is an important family and religious occasion.

For many Jewish families the Sabbath day begins when the mother of the house, who is called 'the foundation of the home', lights two or more candles and says a prayer to welcome the holy day. Young children usually stay at home to help their mother, but the father and older children start the Sabbath day in the synagogue. However, in Progressive synagogues the whole family attends the service. Everyone returns home for the meal, during which the father blesses his children.

weblinks⬝

For more information about the Sabbath day go to:
www.waylinks.co.uk/series/
21stcentury/Judaism

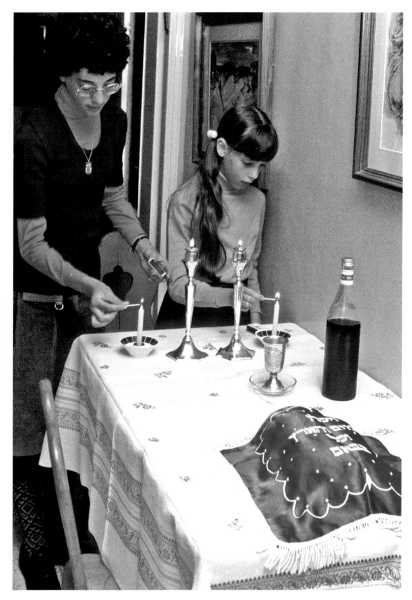

➤ *A Jewish mother and her daughter light the candles that mark the beginning of the Sabbath day. When the male members of the family return home from the service in the synagogue all the family eat the Sabbath meal together.*

Just as the Sabbath day begins with prayer and ceremony, so the day ends with a special ceremony. Traditionally this takes place as soon as three stars can be seen clearly in the sky. The Sabbath day is brought to a close with *Havdalah* ('the separation'), a ceremony that draws a clear line between the holiness of the Sabbath day and the ordinariness of the week ahead. Blessings are given over wine, spices and a plaited candle, as everyone exchanges wishes for a good and 'sweet-smelling' week ahead.

Forbidden activities on the Sabbath day

Many activities are forbidden for Orthodox Jews on the Jewish holy day. They include lighting a fire, cooking, switching on any electrical equipment, playing a musical instrument, driving a car, using public transport such as a bus, train or aeroplane, writing, watching television and riding a bicycle or motorcycle.

◀ *This ornate silver holder contains sweet spices such as cinnamon, cloves, nutmeg and bay leaves. It is used during the Havdalah ceremony which marks the end of the Sabbath day, and the separation of the holy day from the world of work.*

Worship in the synagogue

As Jews enter a synagogue, a place for 'meeting together', some may wash their hands to make themselves fit to worship God before saying a prayer: 'I will worship facing towards your holy Temple. Lord, I love the dwelling of your house and the place where your glory rests.' In many Orthodox synagogues, there must be a minimum of ten men present in the synagogue before a service can go ahead. In Progressive synagogues where this rule is observed, women are included in the total.

Special clothes

Many Orthodox Jewish men wear a skullcap (*kippah*) all of the time, both inside and outside the synagogue. In Orthodox synagogues men also wear over their clothes a special rectangular prayer shawl, called a *tallit*, which is usually made from wool or silk. The tallit has a fringe and tassels at both ends to help worshippers remember the 613 commandments found in the Torah.

For weekday services in the synagogue, Orthodox Jewish men wear two small leather boxes called tefillin, which are tied with leather straps in the middle of the forehead and on the left arm. Like a mezuzah (see page 26), these boxes carry the first two paragraphs of the Shema written on parchment scrolls, reminding each worshipper that the word of God should be carried in their mind and heart.

The words inside a tefillin can be written only by trained scribes using special materials. Once every three years, a tefillin should be opened by a rabbi and the words checked. If the parchment is undamaged, then the words can be corrected if they have become difficult to read. However, if the parchment scroll has been damaged or if it is cracked, then it must be replaced.

▼ *Tallits hanging on a rack in the New Haven Hebrew Day School, Orange, Connecticut, USA. A tallit is a very important personal possession, and many Jewish men are buried with their tallits when they die.*

The rabbi

A rabbi is a person who is well-respected in the Jewish community because he or she is highly trained in the Torah as well as in Jewish law and tradition. In Orthodox synagogues a rabbi is always male, but in Reform, Conservative and other synagogues, rabbis can be either male or female. The rabbi takes part in Sabbath worship by leading prayers, reading from the Torah and giving a sermon. He or she also conducts weddings, funerals and classes to educate members of the community about their religion, as well as visiting the sick and the bereaved.

Three rabbis in an area form a Bet Din. This is a court of Jewish law. This court authorizes marriages and conversions, resolves disputes and interprets matters of Jewish law. It also plays an important part in granting a bill of divorce, called a get, to Jewish couples who want to split up. The get provides couples with a 'religious' divorce which means that they can remarry in a synagogue. Without this, their remarriage is not religiously recognized.

▼ The rabbi has an important part to play in the life of a Jewish community. Here Rabbi Yaakov Rapoport and his helpers knead and roll matzoh in a model bakery in the Jewish Community Center in Dewitt, USA. The matzoh, unleavened bread, plays an important part in the celebrations of Passover.

Jewish festivals

There are many Jewish festivals that are celebrated throughout the year. Among the main festivals are *Rosh Hashanah*, *Yom Kippur*, Sukkot, Shavuot, *Hanukkah*, Purim and Passover.

Rosh Hashanah

Rosh Hashanah is the Jewish New Year and is the most solemn of all the Jewish festivals. It begins the Ten Days of Penitence which is ended by Yom Kippur (the Day of Atonement). It is a time for Jews to reflect on their behaviour in the past year, and to try to right any wrongs they may have done. During Rosh Hashanah a ram's horn, called a *shofar*, is blown one hundred times in the synagogue to call the people to repent of their sins. There are three basic sounds blown: a long, drawn-out note, briefer notes and very short notes. The sound of the shofar reminds Jews of a person crying and helps them to reflect on their own sins and shortcomings.

Yom Kippur

Yom Kippur, a day of prayer and fasting, lasts for 25 hours and draws the festival of Rosh Hashanah to a close. On this day Jews follow the example of God's angels who, according to tradition, do not eat or drink. Jews spend the time in prayer and confession, asking God's forgiveness. They also seek the forgiveness of their friends and relations.

▼ *A rabbi practises blowing a shofar. The shofar is blown one hundred times during the festival of Rosh Hashanah to express the sorrow of the Jewish people for their sins.*

➤ *A booth built for the festival of Sukkot in Jerusalem. This is a public booth, but many people construct and decorate their own booths to celebrate this festival.*

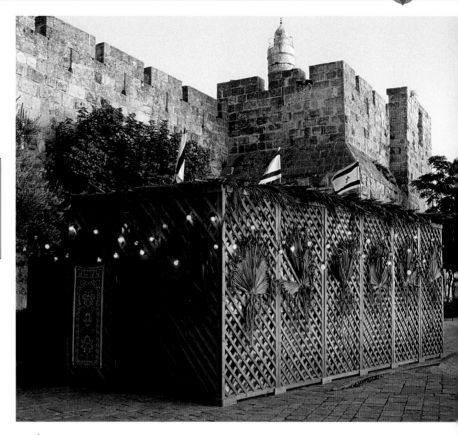

weblinks

To find out the dates of the main Jewish festivals for the coming year, go to:
www.waylinks.co.uk/series/
21stcentury/Judaism

Sukkot

Sukkot is a very happy Jewish festival for which many families build a booth in their garden. This booth is a hut decorated with flowers and fruit, with a roof made of leaves and branches. Many families eat their meals in the booth, and some even sleep in it. The booth is a symbol of trust in the God who protected the Israelites during forty years of travelling in the wilderness (see page 12). During synagogue services, people wave palm branches, myrtle and willow leaves as well as a type of citrus fruit called an *etrog* (used as an early Jewish symbol) to show that God is everywhere.

Shavuot

Shavuot is a summer festival that celebrates the anniversary of God giving the Torah to Moses. Jews decorate their synagogues with lots of flowers to remind worshippers of the tradition that Mount Sinai burst into flower when the Torah was given by God (see page 20). This festival is also known as the Feast of Weeks because it falls seven weeks after the first day of Passover (a 'week of weeks').

In our own words

"*I love Sukkot because I enjoy building a booth in the garden with my parents, brother and sister. The most important festival, though, is that of Pesach because of what it means for all Jews. It is the festival of freedom. We remember that God brought all of our ancestors out of Egypt – the place of slavery. We need to remember that we are descended from slaves as this makes us appreciate our freedom. Then there is seder night. This is a big family gathering. Although we sometimes disagree I get on with my family very well.*"

Amroth, aged 16, Israel

Hanukkah

This festival, also known as the Festival of Light, celebrates the victory of a Jewish family called the Maccabees over the armies of the Syrian king, Antiochus Epiphanes, in the 2nd century BCE. The king's forces had defiled the Temple, making it unfit for worship. When the Temple was repaired, the Jews decided to hold a dedication ceremony. But there was only one flask of oil for lighting the lamp that burns in front of the Ark (see page 9) – sufficient for one night. Miraculously, it lasted for eight days – enough time for new oil to be prepared. Hannukah commemorates the miracle of the oil.

Each day during this festival a candle is lit on a special branched candlestick, until all eight are shining on the last night (see picture page 4). During this festival, children play a Hanukkah game with a spinning top and families eat special potato cakes.

Purim

Purim celebrates the story of Esther who foiled a plot to destroy the Jewish people about 2,500 years ago. This is an exciting festival for children. In the synagogue, the story behind the festival is read out from a decorated scroll and children dress up in the costumes of the characters. Every time the name Haman (the villain in the story) is mentioned, the children make as much noise as possible using whistles, rattles and dustbin lids – or by just stamping their feet! They are trying to blot out the name of Haman with their noise.

Passover

Passover (Pesach) commemorates events that took place over 3,000 years ago, and is the most important of all the Jewish festivals. The Israelites had been slaves in Egypt for over 400 years when God miraculously delivered them

◄ *Children in Jerusalem dressed up for the festival of Purim. The costumes represent characters from the story of Esther. The children parade through the streets before going into the synagogue to hear the story read out.*

(see page 12). The word 'Passover' refers to the time when the Angel of Death passed over the houses of the Jews who had marked their doors with lamb's blood. The Angel of Death spared the Jews but delivered plagues on the Egyptians until the Pharaoh released them. This is why the freedom of people everywhere is the theme of this festival.

The main part of Passover is a special meal, called *seder*, at which the story of the Israelites' slavery and escape is told as the meal is eaten. The seder plate in the middle of the table contains different foods, each of which have a symbolic meaning (see box). They are eaten to help people share in the original experience. Jews also eat unleavened bread at the Passover to remind them that when the Israelites left Egypt, they did not have time to take yeast with them to make their bread rise.

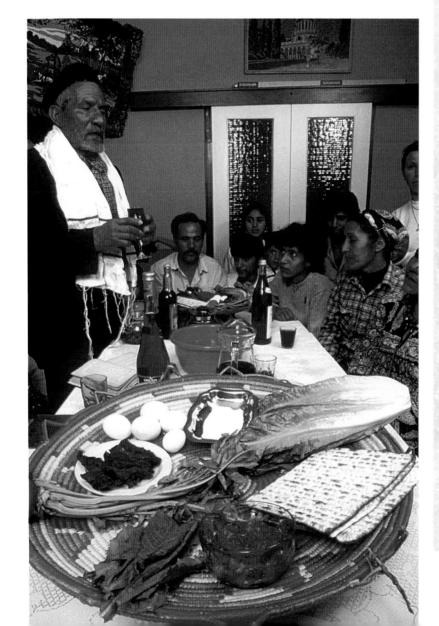

▼ *A seder plate. Most of the food on the plate is eaten during the Passover service to remind worshippers of what happened to the early Israelites.*

The seder plate

The seder plate on the table holds a number of different food items to remind everyone of the meaning of Passover. Two of them, a roasted egg and a roasted lamb bone, commemorate worship in the old Temple, but they are not eaten. Among those that are eaten are bitter herbs, a reminder of the bitter lives of the slaves; one or two green vegetables to remind everyone that this is a Spring festival; and a mixture of chopped apple, nuts, cinnamon and wine to symbolize the cement used by the Israelite slaves when they were building houses for their Egyptian masters.

5 Being Jewish

Being Jewish affects a person's whole life, from the moment they are born until the time of their death. There are Jewish ceremonies or rituals to mark all of the important times in a person's life.

Circumcision

Circumcision is the oldest Jewish religious practice that is still carried out today. It goes all the way back to Abraham who was told by God to circumcise all the male members of his family. It has always been carried out on the eighth day after a boy's birth. The ceremony must take place on that day even if it falls on the Sabbath, since only illness is allowed to delay it. The ceremony, in which the foreskin of a boy's penis is removed, is carried out in the child's home by a *mohel* who does not need to be a rabbi or a doctor, but must be a specially trained religious Jew.

▼ *A Jewish baby boy is circumcised. The operation is performed by a trained person called a mohel and is usually watched by all the members of the family, except the child's mother.*

Bar Mitzvah

Bar Mitzvah marks a boy's entry into adulthood. It is held on the first Sabbath day after a boy's thirteenth birthday, by which time he must be able to read Hebrew well. Until this point in the boy's life, the child's father has been responsible for his son's spiritual welfare and ensuring that the Jewish laws are obeyed. Now this responsibility is passed to the boy himself. As part of his Bar Mitzvah service, a boy must be able to read a passage from the Torah scroll in Hebrew. He also leads the congregation in their prayers.

Bat Mitzvah

Girls join adult Jewish society a year earlier than boys. In some non-Orthodox synagogues they have a similar ceremony, called *Bat Mitzvah*, in which girls read from the Torah. In many Orthodox synagogues there is a ceremony for girls in which, although they do not read publicly from the Torah, they do give a special talk about the Bible reading for that week.

In our own words

"I have just celebrated my Bar Mitzvah. I learned Hebrew in our classes at the synagogue – although it is frightening to stand up in front of all your relations and friends to read from the Torah in a language that is not your native tongue! I'd practised it a lot, however, and all went well. The service was followed by a special meal at which everyone gave me presents – that was very nice! I stood up to thank them for their love and kindness as well as telling them my hopes for a Jewish future. I want to be able to keep as many of the Jewish laws as possible, to live a life that is faithful to God and to establish my own Jewish home in the years to come."

Joseph, 13, England

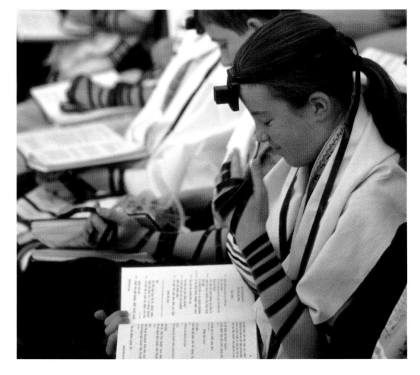

◄ *A Bar Mitzvah class is held for both boys and girls in a Conservative synagogue in Tel Aviv, Israel. In this class, children are taught Hebrew as well as more about their Jewish faith.*

Marriage

Marriage is very important to all Jews. Although a Jewish marriage, for which both bride and groom have to be Jewish, does not have to take place in a synagogue, it is most likely to be held in a place of worship.

During the wedding service the bride and groom stand together under a *chuppah* (canopy) which is sometimes decorated with white flowers. This canopy is a symbol of the home that the couple are going to set up together. The couple drink wine together as the wedding blessings are recited. The groom gives his bride a ring and formally takes her in marriage. In Progressive services, the bride takes the groom in marriage as well. Then the *ketubah*, the marriage certificate, is read aloud and signed before the groom crushes a wine glass beneath his feet. This is an ancient practice recalling the destruction of the Temple, which Jews remember even in times of great joy.

Judaism encourages a Jew to marry someone who is also Jewish. Many Jews believe that Judaism is so centred around home life that unless a married couple share the same religious background and beliefs, it will be very difficult for them to live together in true harmony.

▼ *A Jewish couple stand beneath a chuppah at their wedding. A Jewish wedding can take place out of doors, in the synagogue or in the home.*

Death

Jewish tradition demands that a Jewish funeral and burial take place as soon as possible after death – ideally within 24 hours. Funeral services must be simple, with the body being placed in a basic coffin. This is because Jews believe that everyone, rich and poor, is equal in death since there is no difference between them in the eyes of God. Orthodox Jews do not allow cremation, although it is permitted by Progressive Jews.

For a week after the burial, friends and relations meet in the home of the dead person to comfort one another. During this time close relatives of the deceased are not expected to go to work or to do anything in the home so that they can grieve without worrying about the everyday details of their lives. Friends and relations support them in every way. For almost a year, close relatives recite the *kaddish*, a holy prayer, every day. A special candle is lit each year on the anniversary of the person's death.

The kaddish

This prayer praises God who is the giver of all life. It contains these words:
'Let us magnify and let us sanctify the great name of God in the world which he created according to his will. May his kingdom come in your lifetime, and in your days, and in the lifetime of the family of Israel – quickly and speedily may it come... He is far beyond any blessing or song, any honour or any consolation that can be spoken of in this world.'

▼ *A girl lights a memorial candle at the grave of the assassinated Jewish Prime Minister, Yitzak Rabin.*

✡ 5 Judaism in today's world

Judaism is a very old religion. Like other religions, however, it needs to be able to face modern problems in the world. To do this it takes the principles of the Torah and tries to see how those principles can be applied today.

Justice for everyone

Jews believe that God gave all people the laws they need to live good and honest lives when he gave Moses the Torah on Mount Sinai. The Torah contains everything that Jews need to know about how they should behave and what is expected of them by God. A legal code has been drawn up from the Torah by rabbis over the centuries and this is called the *Halakhah*. Jews believe that these laws can bring justice for everyone.

Jews believe that if everyone was to take notice of the advice in the Torah to 'love your neighbour as you love yourself' (Leviticus 19:18) then everything would be well in the world. People, however, have been given free will by God, and many choose not to obey God's laws. The Torah says that those who break these laws must be held responsible for their actions. When they are punished, Jews believe that people are not only paying for their crimes but also acting as deterrents to other possible criminals.

The death penalty

The ultimate punishment for the most serious crimes is death, and the Torah lists those crimes for which the punishment should be death by hanging or stoning. As the Torah says: 'The principle is a life for a life' (Leviticus 24:17-18). This means that if someone takes another life they should surrender their own. In fact, although this was laid down in the Torah, people were rarely put to death in ancient Israel. A murderer could only be executed if there were two independent witnesses to the crime that he or she had committed – and only if the murderer fully understood the consequences of his or her actions. These conditions were almost impossible to meet.

Modern Israel abolished the death penalty for almost all crimes in the 1950s. Only one person has been executed since 1948, when

Choosing judges

These standards are set down for judges in the Torah:
'Appoint judges and officials for each of your tribes in every town the Lord your God is giving you, and they shall judge the people fairly. Do not pervert justice or show partiality. Do not accept a bribe, for a bribe blinds the eyes of the wise and twists the words of the righteous. Follow justice and justice alone, so that you may live and possess the land the Lord your God is giving you.'

(Deuteronomy 16:18-20)

the modern State of Israel was set up. This happened in 1963 when Adolf Eichmann, a leading Nazi, was found guilty of murdering thousands of Jews during the Holocaust in the Second World War (see page 16). He was executed because his crime was considered to be so horrific that only the death sentence was suitable.

Remembering the Holocaust

When the Second World War ended in 1945 and the Allied soldiers liberated the survivors of the Nazi death camps (see page 42), the horror of the Holocaust was revealed to the world. People were deeply shocked. As the truth of the mass murders was gradually pieced together, both Jews and non-Jews became extremely concerned that these events should never be forgotten. In this way it was hoped that the Holocaust could never happen again.

▼ *The Jewish Museum in Berlin was designed by the Polish architect Daniel Libeskind and opened in 2001. The building is in the shape of a long zig-zag, partly based on the idea of an opened Star of David. It celebrates the achievements of German Jews as well as commemorating the Holocaust, and the millions who died under Nazi rule.*

Anti-Semitism and racism

For centuries Jews have found themselves to be the victims of prejudice (see page 15). In the case of Jews this prejudice is called anti-Semitism – hatred directed against Jews simply because they are Jews. Jews have often found themselves to be the butt of jokes about their religious traditions, beliefs, ways of worshipping and clothing. In more extreme cases Jewish graves, kosher shops and synagogues have been defaced, vandalised and attacked. In recent years there has been a growth in anti-Semitism in Europe.

Racism

Prejudice is not something that happens only to Jews. All groups of people suffer from prejudice – the disabled, the old, homosexuals and black people among them. They are picked on because they are in some way 'different' and stand out from other people. At its worst, prejudice can grow into hatred, harassment and violence. When it involves hatred of a whole race it is called 'racism'.

Foreigners

This advice comes from the Torah: 'When an alien [foreigner] lives with you in your land, do not ill-treat him. The alien living with you must be treated as one of your native-born. Love him as yourself, for you were aliens in Egypt. I am the Lord your God.'
(Leviticus 19:33-34)

Jews believe that racism is wrong because all people were created and so are valued by God. They believe that to discriminate against a person is to deny that the person is part of God's good creation. As the Torah says: 'God created human beings, making them to be like himself' (Genesis 1:27).

Jews believe that if people are made by God, and are like God, it is wrong to hate them. If everyone has been created to serve God in their own different ways then all religions, and people, must be accepted for what they are. The teachings of the Torah explained this long ago and, having often been the victims of persecution themselves, Jews strongly believe that it is wrong to mistreat anyone just because they are different.

◄ *Jewish prisoners in Dachau concentration camp in Germany cheer their American liberators at the end of the Second World War, in May 1945.*

In our own words

"I am a Jew. Other people know that I am a Jew and they accept me for what I am. That goes for all my friends. I have not suffered from anti-Semitism but I do know people who have. I have also read in the newspapers of anti-Semitic acts which have been carried out in many other countries. This worries me a lot. I do not understand why people cannot leave us alone. Why do many people hate the Jews so much?"

Rebecca, aged 17, USA

▼ *A woman looks at desecrated Jewish graves at a cemetery in St Petersburg, Russia, in February 2004. In this attack, the gravestones were daubed with the swastika symbol used by the Nazis. There has been a rise in anti-Semitism in most European countries in recent years.*

Wealth and poverty

The simple fact that some people are very rich while others have barely enough to survive has always upset people. The Torah, though, is quite realistic about this (see box). Jews believe that it is God who decides who will be rich and who will be poor. They believe that there will always be rich and poor people in the world.

The rich and the poor

In the Jewish Scriptures is quite acceptable for someone to be rich, but it is not acceptable for them to dedicate themselves simply to making more and more money. Judaism teaches that everyone has a duty to help the poor since no-one chooses to be poor. As the Talmud teaches: 'Poverty is worse than fifty plagues.' At festival times, money should be given so that the poor can join in with the celebrations as well.

The Hebrew Scriptures give practical advice as to how the poor could be helped and slaves freed in ancient times. They say that at harvest time farmers should leave corn growing at the edges of their fields for the poor to collect. Fruits such as grapes and olives that were missed at the first picking should be left. Every seventh year, when a field is left fallow, poor people and wildlife can take what grows. Any slaves must be given their freedom after they have served their masters for six years.

The poor in Jewish Scriptures

'There will always be poor people in the land. Therefore I command you to be open-handed towards your brothers and towards the poor and needy in your land.' (Deuteronomy 15:11)

'When God gives any man wealth and possessions and enables him to enjoy them, to accept his lot and be happy in his work – this is a gift of God.' (Ecclesiastes 5:19)

'Naked a man comes from his mother's womb, and as he comes, so he departs. He takes nothing from his labour that he can carry in his hand.' (Ecclesiastes 5:15)

▼ Jewish charity boxes. The money collected was once used to buy land in Israel but is now mostly used to provide clean drinking water for that country.

Tzedaka

The teaching of the Jewish Scriptures is that everyone should give ten per cent of their income (a tithe) to the poor. Even someone who has received charity because they are poor is expected to give part of it away to other poor people. The word *tzedaka* literally means 'justice', and giving a tithe is a fair and right thing to do. Because no-one likes receiving charity in person, Jews usually give their tzedaka to a charity. Then a poor person can receive their rightful share of God's goodness without knowing who gave them the money. It is very important in the Jewish community that the poor should retain their self-respect at all times.

'Operation Solomon'

For centuries a community of up to 500,000 Jews lived in the northern province of Gondar in Ethiopia, isolated from the rest of the Jewish world. This community called itself Beta Israel – the 'house of Israel'. In the 17th century, Beta Israel fought for its independence from Christian Ethiopians, but without success. Only in the 19th century did Beta Israel start to make links with the worldwide community of Jews. In the 1970s, anti-Semitism became an increasing problem in Gondar, and many Jews wanted to leave for Israel, but were prevented by the Ethiopian government. Terrible famines in the 1980s led Israel to mount several 'rescue' operations for Ethiopian Jews. In 1984 and 1985 almost 8,000 Jews were rescued and brought to Israel. In the following five years, more Jews were taken from Ethiopia, but nearly all of those left behind were elderly, women and children. Then, in 1991, as rebel forces threatened the Ethiopian capital Addis Ababa, a secret Israeli airlift rescued over 14,000 Jews from Ethiopia. This was known as 'Operation Solomon'. There are now 36,000 Ethiopian Jews living in Israel.

▶ *An Israeli leads a group of Ethiopian Jews to a waiting plane at Addis Ababa airport on 25 May 1991, during 'Operation Solomon'. The Israeli government authorized a special permit for the Israeli airline, El Al, in order for the airlift to take place on the Jewish Sabbath.*

Glossary

Abraham The Israelite patriarch who was the first to believe in one God. He was given the promise by God that his descendants would inherit the land of Israel.

anti-Semitism Hatred and prejudice directed towards people because they are Jews.

Ark The cupboard in a synagogue in which the Torah is kept.

Bar mitzvah ('son of the commandment') The ceremony in the synagogue to mark the time when a Jewish boy becomes an adult – after his 13th birthday. The boy reads from the Torah in Hebrew and starts to wear his tefillin for daily prayers.

Bat mitzvah ('daughter of the commandment') The ceremony in the synagogue to mark a girl's entry into adulthood.

bimah The reading-desk in a synagogue from which the Torah is read and the sermon delivered on the Sabbath day.

chuppah A canopy under which a wedding service takes place. It symbolizes the home that the couple are setting up together.

covenant The agreement made between God and Abraham upon which Judaism is based.

Diaspora Communities of Jews who settled outside Israel.

Exodus The journey of the Israelites out of Egyptian slavery towards Canaan, their Promised Land.

Halakhah The Jewish legal code that has been drawn up from the Torah.

Hanukkah (Festival of Light) A festival that celebrates the victory of a Jewish family called the Maccabees and the miracle of the oil in the Temple.

Havdalah The ceremony that marks the end of the Sabbath day.

Hebrew The language in which the Jewish Scriptures are written and in which most services in the synagogue are conducted.

kaddish A prayer that praises God as the giver of life.

ketubah A marriage certificate.

kippah A skullcap, worn by Orthodox Jewish men.

kosher The word applied to the food that Jews are allowed to eat and also to the way in which that food must be prepared.

menorah The seven-branched candlestick found in a synagogue.

Mesopotamia ('land between two rivers') The ancient region between the rivers Tigris and Euphrates that is today part of modern Iraq.

Messiah ('the anointed one') For Jews it means a great leader who will be sent by God to deliver them from their enemies and bring all of the world to an understanding of God.

mezuzah A casing that holds a tiny scroll on which is written the first two paragraphs of the Shema. A mezuzah is attached to the right-hand doorpost of most rooms in a Jewish house.

mohel The Jewish professional employed to circumcise Jewish boys on the eighth day after birth.

Moses The man who led the Israelites out of slavery and received the Torah from God on Mount Sinai.

Passover (Pesach) A festival that commemorates the delivery of the Israelites out of Egypt.

patriarch One of three founding fathers of the Jewish people – Abraham, Isaac and Jacob.

prophet Someone who is believed to have received messages from God.

Purim A festival that celebrates the story of Esther, who foiled a plot to destroy the Jewish people about 2,500 years ago.

Rabbi The title given to an authorized teacher in Judaism.

Rosh Hashanah The Jewish New Year and the start of the Ten Days of Penitence.

Sabbath day (Shabbat) The seventh day of the week, the day of rest. In the Jewish Scriptures it was the day on which God rested from creating the world. It is also a weekly reminder of God's rescuing the Israelites from Egyptian slavery.

seder The special meal that forms the main part of Passover.

Shavuot A festival that celebrates the giving of the Torah by God to Moses.

Shekhina God's presence or closeness.

Shema ('hear') The Jewish name for the words of Deuteronomy 6:4. The Shema is recited twice each day by Jews as a statement of their faith in God.

shofar A ram's horn.

Sukkot A festival that commemorates the time that the Jews spent travelling through the wilderness to their 'Promised Land' of Canaan.

synagogue The Jewish meeting place for prayer, study and instruction in the Scriptures.

tallit A prayer shawl.

tefillin Small boxes containing biblical texts which are fixed to the foreheads and left arms of Jewish men during prayer.

Temple The Jewish Temple in Jerusalem was first built by Solomon around 950BCE and destroyed by the Babylonians in 586BCE.

Ten Commandments The law code delivered by God to Moses on Mount Sinai. The first four are religious laws and the other six are social.

Tenakh The name given to the Jewish Scriptures made up of the Torah, the Prophets and the Writings.

Torah Jews use this word to mean two different things. It can be translated as 'law' when it applies particularly to the 'law of Moses' – the first five books of the Jewish Scriptures. It is also used to mean 'teaching'.

tzedaka ('justice') The giving of money to those less fortunate.

Yom Kippur The Day of Atonement that brings Rosh Hashanah to a close.

Zionist The movement in the 19th and 20th centuries which aimed at founding a Jewish state in Palestine.

Timeline

BCE	
2000-1900	Time of the Biblical patriarchs – Abraham, Isaac and Jacob
1600s	Israelites go into slavery
1200s-1100s	Moses leads the Israelites out of slavery and receives the Torah and the Ten Commandments. The Israelites conquer Canaan
c.1000	King David unites the tribes in Jerusalem
c.960	Solomon succeeds David and builds the first Temple
c.920	Solomon dies and his kingdom divides into Israel in the north and Judah in the south
722	Israel conquered by the Assyrians
586	Judah falls to the Babylonians. Temple in Jerusalem destroyed and Jewish population deported
167	Judas Maccabeous leads a revolt against the Greeks
63	Pompey conquers Palestine. Jewish communities spread throughout Roman Empire
40-4	Romans put Herod the Great on the throne of Judea

CE	
66-70	Jews revolt against the Romans. Romans destroy the Temple built by Herod the Great in Jerusalem
638	Muslims conquer Jerusalem
1066	Jews settle in England
1290	Jews expelled from England
1306	Jews expelled from parts of France
1348	The Black Death: Jews are blamed and massacred throughout Europe
1492	Spanish Jews given choice of conversion to Christianity or to leave Spain
1497	Jews expelled from Portugal
1881-2	Jews persecuted in Russia
1917	Balfour Declaration to establish Jewish homeland in the state of Palestine
1939-45	Second World War: six million Jews killed in Holocaust
1948	Founding of State of Israel
1967	The 'Six-Day War' between Israel and Egypt, Syria and Jordan
1979	Peace treaty between Israel and Egypt

Further reading

This is Judaism by Michael Keene (Nelson Thornes, 1996)

What do we know about Judaism? by Doreen Fine (Hodder Wayland, 1995)

The Jewish Experience by Liz Aylett (Hodder and Stoughton, 2000)

Foundations in R.E. Judaism 'Core' and 'Essential' editions by Ina Taylor (Nelson Thornes, 2000)

Believers in One God by Michael Keene (Cambridge University Press, 1993)

Examining Four Religions by Michael Keene (Harper Collins, 1997)

Judaism by Arye Forte (Hodder and Stoughton, 1989)

Index